LEAN STONE PUBLISHING

"Turn the Page And Live a Better Life"

www.leanstonebookclub.com

© **Copyright 2017 Lean Stone Publishing - All rights reserved.**

In no way is it legal to reproduce, duplicate, or transmit any part of this document in either electronic means or in printed format. Recording of this publication is strictly prohibited and any storage of this document is not allowed unless with written permission from the publisher. All rights reserved.

The information provided herein is stated to be truthful and consistent, in that any liability, in terms of inattention or otherwise, by any usage or abuse of any policies, processes, or directions contained within is the solitary and utter responsibility of the recipient reader. Under no circumstances will any legal responsibility or blame be held against the publisher for any reparation, damages, or monetary loss due to the information herein, either directly or indirectly.

Respective authors own all copyrights not held by the publisher.

Legal Notice:

This book is copyright protected. This is only for personal use. You cannot amend, distribute, sell, use, quote or paraphrase any part or the content within this book without the consent of the author or copyright owner. Legal action will be pursued if this is breached.

Disclaimer Notice:

Please note the information contained within this document is for educational and entertainment purposes only. Every attempt has been made to provide accurate, up to date and reliable complete information. No warranties of any kind are expressed or implied. Readers acknowledge that the author is not engaging in the rendering of legal, financial, medical or professional advice.

By reading this document, the reader agrees that under no circumstances are we responsible for any losses, direct or indirect, which are incurred as a result of the use of information contained within this document, including, but not limited to, —errors, omissions, or inaccuracies.

India

History of India: From Prehistoric Settlements to the Modern Republic of India

Table of Contents

Introduction 6

Chapter 1 – Ancient India 8

Chapter 2 – Medieval India 18

Chapter 3 – British Colonization + East India Company 32

Chapter 4 – India from 1949 Until the Present 41

Chapter 5 – Indian Politics and Its Role in the World Today 50

Chapter 6 – Indian Culture and Religion 60

Chapter 7 – Delhi + Things to See in India 71

Conclusion 75

Introduction

PROBABLY THE BEST BOOK CLUB ONLINE...

"If you love books. You will love the Lean Stone Book Club."
*** Exclusive Deals That Any Book Fan Would Love! ***

Visit leanstonebookclub.com/join

(IT'S FREE)!

"India is the cradle of human race, the birthplace of human speech, the mother of history, the grandmother of legend, and the great-grandmother of tradition. Our most valuable and most instructive materials are treasured up in India only." (Mark Twain)

This quote perfectly summarizes the essence of India, its culture, and its history. The truth is that few countries on Earth have had such an unprecedented pace of development.

India is the place of creativity, is the place of numerous cultures and religions, tongues and races. It represents a unique combination of elements that distinguish it from other nations.

Fortified by constant flows of migration and marauders from other lands, each of them has influenced, to some extent, the Indian's perception of life. India's culture teaches us about the gentleness of the human mind, tolerance, and the importance of promoting an understanding spirit and a pacifying love towards all humans.

In this book, we will briefly present the predominant aspects that shaped India and made it turn into what it is today – the largest democratic country in the world whose unity in diversity concept makes it stand out.

We will take you on a discovery journey starting from ancient India, medieval India, the colonization, its political approach and place in the world, indicating how this country continues to evolve in spite of all the hardships it surpassed throughout the centuries.

How did everything start? What are the very grounds of the Indian society? What are the primary elements that shape their culture and what makes it so special and unique? This brief book aims at answering these questions and many others, enhancing your understanding of India.

Chapter 1 - Ancient India

India's history is a compelling epic of a unique civilization. The name *India,* in truth, is derived from the Indus River. In the famous Indian epic *Mahabharata,* the name *Bharata* appears, which makes reference to the ancient mythological emperor.

Based on Puranas (historical/religious texts) originating from the 5th century CE, Bharata was the one that conquered the entire sub-continent of India, governing the land in harmony and peace. Consequently, the land was given the name Bharatavarsha – which means the sub-continent of Bharata.

Considering that the hominid activity in the Indian sub-continent goes back to 250,000 years, it is considered one of the oldest inhabited places on Earth. Numerous archaeological evacuations have brought to the light valuable artifacts used by early humans – stone tools included. This indicates a quite early date for human habitation in the region.

The Vedic Period (c.1700 – 150 BCE)

Around 1500 BCE, the Indo-European people migrated to India. Apart from bringing their spoken language, they also brought their religious beliefs with them.

It is believed that the Aryan influence has determined the rise of the Vedic Period in India. This timeframe is featured by a rural lifestyle, and the locals' devotement to the religious texts known as *The Vedas*. These collect a conglomeration of songs and stories related to Hinduism.

Although the religious beliefs that were typical of the Vedic period are thought to be much older, it was during this timeframe that these ideas were recognized as the religion of *Sanatan Dharma,* whose translation is *Eternal Order,* today referred to as Hinduism. A fundamental doctrine of Hinduism is that there is purpose and order in the universe and every human's life. If one accepts this order, he/she will live life properly.

This belief was perfectly illustrated in the Vedic period, as during that time, the society flourished considerably. Governments have been institutionalized, and significant social customs were fully integrated into the locals' everyday lives.

During the 6th century BCE, religious reformers Siddhartha Gautama and Vardhaman Mahvira created two religions, namely Buddhism and Jainism, in this way breaking away from Hinduism. These religious changes played an important part in the cultural and social turmoil, which was accompanied by the establishment of city-states and the rise of grand kingdoms – an example would be the Kingdom of Magadha under Bimbisara's government.

The urbanization and civilization raised the attention of Cyrus, the ruler of the Persian Empire. As a result, he invaded India in 530 BCE, initiating a campaign that aimed at conquering the flourishing region. In ten years' time, India was led firmly by Darius I, controlling the regions we know today as Pakistan and Afghanistan. An immediate consequence was the adaptation of Indian and Persian religious beliefs.

People and Society in Ancient India

In Ancient India, people were typically healthy and fit and pursued various skills and occupations. That is widely attributed to the availability of various means of sustenance and the abundance of fresh drinking water. The land was fertile and had a wide variety of trees, crops, and plants. Apart from that, metals such as gold, copper, silver, and iron were extensively used in order to create weapons, ornaments, jewelry, shields and other useful articles.

The social structure of the time included seven castes, without promoting oppression or gradation. At that time, there weren't any slaves in the Indian society, as the individual freedom of each man was respected.

The writings from that time highlight a well-functioning, well-established society that has flourished over an extensive period to accomplish its status.

Nevertheless, by the time of Hiuen Tsang (7th century), the social structure has changed, becoming a bit more rigid, noting a range of divisions between castes in terms of behaviors and styles. Still, irrespective of this change, no instance of conflict, harassment or oppression has been noted.

Another noteworthy element that featured the society at that time was the significance of the right functioning of the army. Generally, the art of warfare was taught to kids from an early age. Only the bravest and strongest could enter the military service.

The Great Empires of Ancient India

Persia ruled over northern India until Alexander the Great conquered the land in 327 BCE. One year after that, Alexander took the next step by defeating the Achaemenid Empire, in this way conquering the entire Indian subcontinent. Once again, this change brought a mixture of foreign influences, which determined the rise of the Greco-Buddhist culture. This had a notable impact on all cultural areas in Northern India, from the way people dressed to religion and art.

Relics and statues from this period indicate Buddha and other important figures, and the typical Hellenic pose and dress were commonly met.

After Alexander's departure from India, a new era begins – the era of the Mauryan Empire (322 – 185 BCE), being ruled by Chandragupta Maurya, the first emperor of the Mauryan Empire.

Beforehand, India included a small number of independent states, except the Magadha Kingdom, which was governed by the Nanda dynasty. In this respect, Chandragupta would be the first one that would unify India. Chandragupta's son, Bindusara, expanded the empire, his reign being followed by Ashoka the Great, under whose reign the land attained supremacy from numerous points of views.

For starters, he took action by conquering the Eastern city-state of Kalinga. However, this action resulted in the death of approximately 100,000 people. Being appalled by the level of destruction and death his action brought, he turned to the teachings of Buddha, in this way promoting Buddhist principles and teachings. As a result, he constructed numerous Buddhist monasteries, donating to Buddhist communities.

Nonetheless, his devotement determined a strain in the government, from both political and financial points of view. His grandson – Sampadi, didn't see eye to eye with him on the matter. What is more, by the end of his reign, due to his regular religious donations, the government treasury exhausted. After his death, the decline of the empire followed.

The country was divided into smaller empires and kingdoms – this timeframe became known as the *Middle Period*. During this period, the trade with Rome increased, being followed by Augustus Caesar's conquering of Egypt in 30 BC. Before, Egypt would be India's prime trade partner. This time monitored exceptional individual and cultural developments, which is why this is thought to be the Golden Age of India – under the reign of Gupta Empire.

The founder of the Gupta Empire was Sri Gupta (240-280 CE). It is believed that he was part of the merchant class, which makes his rise to power rather unusual for the time being. His reign would stabilize India from numerous points of view. Domains such as mathematics, technology, architecture, literature, philosophy, science, engineering, astronomy, religion, art and many other were revolutionized at that time. This resulted in some of the most notable achievements of the era.

Furthermore, the *Puranas of Vysa* were created during this period, just as the renowned caves of Ellora and Ajanta, featuring beautiful vaulted rooms and unique carvings. Aryabhatta, the eminent mathematician, discovered the significance of the concept of zero, which he is given credit to have invented. Concurrently, Varahamihira aimed at exploring the vast domain of astronomy.

Considering that the founder of the Gupta Empire wasn't an advocate of Hinduism, it is not wrong to say that Gupta Rulers promoted Buddhism as the official, national belief. As a result, on sites such as Ellora and Ajanta, there is a multitude of Buddhist artwork, instead of Hindu artwork.

The Decline of an Empire and the Beginning of Islam

Due to a succession of unsuitable leaders, the empire experienced a steady decline, and it collapsed around 550 CE. The rule of Harshavardhan (590-647) replaced the Gupta Empire, who was a well-read man with outstanding achievements. Being a devout Buddhist, he forbade the killing of animals. Nonetheless, he still acknowledged the need to *sometimes* kill in military battle.

Under his reign, the north of India developed beautifully. Still, the kingdom disintegrated after his death. The repeated invasions of the Huns had been successfully held off. Still, after Harshavardhan's death and the fall of the kingdom, their invasion was inevitable. Chaos divided India into a wide range of little states that lacked the power and means to fight against powerful forces.

Another notable moment is when Muslim General

Muhammed bin Quasim subjugated northern India. After the Muslim invasion, independent city-states or communities governed by a city became the standard form of government. In today's region known as modern-day Pakistan, the Islamic Sultanates rose, spreading towards the North West.

As a result, the Islamic Mughal Empire didn't encounter a lot of difficulty in conquering the region. From that point onward, India was influenced, to some degree, by various foreign powers (Portuguese, British, French), until it finally won its independence in 1947 CE.

Misconceptions about Ancient India

Did it ever happen to you to get into an argument regarding a historical aspect? In such situations, it could be rather challenging to pinpoint the truth and make the difference between a false and real affirmation.

On that note, in this section, I will address the most common myths and assumptions regarding ancient India and the Vedic period.

1. Women Were Conveyed as Being Inferior to Men

Without a doubt, this is one of the most widespread misconceptions. In truth, in the Vedic society, women were treated with noteworthy respect. As a result, they were included in both social and domestic works, where they co-operated with men. While their main responsibility was to be respectful wives, they benefited from proper education, as well.

That being said, in the Rig-Vedic age, women such as Ghosa, Mamata, Biswabara and others accomplished proficiency in distinct branches of Scripture or Shastra. What is more, some of these women even became renowned composers of Vedic hymns.

And that is not all, apart from the literary pursuit, women also had the possibility of learning the art of warfare.

As for widow or child marriage, these weren't practiced during that time. The sati burning practice neither. Nevertheless, a common habit at that time was marrying the brother's childless widow. On the whole, the standards of women's moral character were pretty high, and their role in the society was important, contrary to popular belief.

Nevertheless, in the later Vedic period, the women's status was lower than previously. As a result, they didn't have the right to inherit. Apart from that, they didn't have political rights either.

2. In the Early Vedic Period, People Were Discriminated

Discrimination is, until our day, a common concern and source of problems. That being said, it is easy to assume that this was an issue, centuries ago, including in the early Vedic period when the world's countries weren't as civilized as they are today, right? Nevertheless, it appears that in the early Vedic period, there wasn't a caste/color discrimination in the Indian society. The profession wasn't conveyed as something hereditary, and exogamy wasn't frowned upon.

Exogamy refers to the custom of marrying outside of a tribe, community or clan. What is more, there weren't any additional religious or moral restrictions that were imposed on the society.

So, how was the society organized? It was divided into three classes: landed aristocrats and warriors, priests and commonalty.

This division was made to ease the economic and social organization of the Vedic society, which makes sense.

Nevertheless, the color and class discrimination started to

expand as a result of the wars that took place from that point onward. Hence, it appears that the military conflict was the primary root to discriminatory problems.

3. Education Wasn't a Priority in Ancient India

Education has been important in the Indian society since the times of the Vedic civilization. There are two famous renowned universities, which are also known to be the oldest in the world, namely Nalanda University and Takshashila University.

The later was established approximately 2700 years ago. More than 10,500 students came here, from across the world, in order to become specialized in their fields of study. The university provided educational preparation in surgery, politics, agriculture, philosophy, the Vedas, grammar, astronomy, archery, warfare, dance, commerce, music and so on. Chinese travelers make reference to Takshashila University in their writings, which outlines its importance during that time.

As for Nalanda University, it originates from the 5th century. It continued to flourish until the 12th century, being the first university in the world that featured residential quarters for both teachers and students. This university was acknowledged as a first-class learning center, as students from China, Japan, Tibet, Korea, Turkey, Indonesia, and Persia would come to study here.

Nevertheless, due to the Muslim invasion in the 12th century, most universities (Nalanda, Vikramashila, Telhara, Somapura Mahavihara, Odantapuri, and others) were destroyed. Hence, this has led to the decrease of ancient Indian scientific development in astronomy, anatomy, alchemy, and mathematics.

Fun Facts!

Next, I would like to introduce you to a range of interesting facts regarding ancient India. These will definitely broaden your perspective and comprehension.

- Ayurveda is reckoned as the most ancient school of medicine. Additionally, it was developed primarily by Charaka, an eminent Indian physician, during those ancient times. As you probably already know, it is the only system that conveys medicine from a holistic viewpoint.
- Ancient Indians benefited from effective water harvesting. In truth, the first reservoir and dam for irrigation were constructed in Saurashtra.
- Sushruta was a renowned physician in ancient India and conducted challenging surgeries such as fractures, brain surgery, cesareans, and many others.
- Chess was a widespread game and occupation in ancient India. At that time, it was referred to as *Chaturanga,* which meant four members of an army.

If It Were Your Choice

- What would you have done if you were Muslim General Muhammed bin Quasim? Would you have chosen to subjugate India because the country was divided into numerous states? Or would you have chosen otherwise?
- If it were your choice, would you have invaded India in 530 BCE (as Cyrus, the ruler of the Persian Empire chose to do)? What would have influenced your decision and why?

Pop Quiz!

To make sure that you remember the key points mentioned in this chapter, we have prepared the following questions for you!

1. What are the primary characteristics that featured the Vedic Era?
2. What role did religion play in the development of the Indian culture?
3. Which are the main empires of ancient India?
4. What determined the coming of Muslims to India?
5. How did the arrival of the Muslims influence the Indian culture and religious beliefs?

Chapter 2 - Medieval India

The medieval period holds crucial importance in the history of India, as it registered a wide range of developments in the field of languages and art. In addition to that, during this timeframe, the Indian culture was significantly influenced by other religions. The medieval period lasted from the 8th until the 18th century – being divided into two distinct periods: the early medieval period (8th – 13th century) and the late medieval period (13th century – 18th century).

The early medieval period noted a number of wars among regional kingdoms from the south and northern India, while the late medieval period witnessed the invasion of Muslims, Turks, Afghans, and Mughals. Some historians consider that the medieval period in Indian history commenced with the arrival of the Turks, who brought a new religion that changed the Indian society on all levels.

This time witnessed the rise of a number of important dynasties such as the Cholas of Southern India, the Mughals of northern India, the Rajput of western India, and many others. Now we would like to present the most notable aspects of Medieval India.

The Chola Dynasty

Chola Dynasty was one of the leading powers in India who ruled over an extensive timeframe. Originally, their beginnings go as back as the 2nd century BC, and they maintained their power and position until the 13th century.

From the 9th century until the 13th century, the Cholas ruled from Tamilnadu to Southeast Asian nations - Cholamandalam region. Since the beginning of the 9th century, the Chola became the strongest dynasty located in southern India. Their army and navy were powerful and well-prepared.

In addition, during their regime, both Jainism and Buddhism flourished beautifully. Apart from that, areas of fine arts, literature, and metal casting reached new accomplishments. In the 14th century, the establishment of Vijayanagara is noteworthy – also known as Karnataka, this state was the proof of Indian development. There are various inscriptions on temple walls that talk of the functioning and organization of village councils during the Chola Kingdom.

Delhi Sultanates

The Delhi Sultanate was the first Islamic Empire in India's history, ruling from 1206 to 1526. It was made from former Muslim slave-soldiers, known as *Mamluks,* who established the dynasties that ruled in India during that timeframe. In spite of their significant cultural impact, the sultanates weren't that powerful, which is why they didn't last for too long.

Each one of the Delhi Sultanates initiated a process of accommodation and assimilation between the Muslim culture and the traditions and religions of India.

The Mamluk Dynasty was founded in 1206 by Qutub-ud-Dïn Aybak, who was a Central Asian Turk and also a former general for the Ghurid Sultanate – a Persian dynasty of majestic importance that ruled over the territory today occupied by Pakistan, Iran, Afghanistan and Northern India.

Still, his reign was pretty short, and it was his son-in-law, namely Iltutmish, who would actually put the grounds for the sultanate in Delhi.

The second dynasty of the Delhi Sultanates was the Khilji Dynasty. It was named after Jalal-Ud-Din Khilji, as he assassinated the last ruler of the Mamluk dynasty. However, his fate wasn't a lucky one considering that he was killed by his nephew – Ala-ud-Din Khilji, who would become known as a tyrant.

Nonetheless, he was also the one who kept the Mongols from entering India. During his reign, the country experienced a rapid expansion in its Central and Southern parts, where he grew the taxes to increase his treasury and equip his army. Soon after his rule, the dynasty would crumble.

Moving on, the Tughlaq Dynasty managed to keep control over India from 1320 to 1414. Ghiyas-ud-din Tughlaq succeeded in expanding the borders of the dynasty, and they reached the south-eastern coast of modern-day India. This way, India was the largest it would be during the Delhi Sultanates.

However, this didn't last for long, as Timur invaded India in 1398, destroying Delhi and massacring the locals. After the invasion, a family claiming to descend from Prophet Muhammad started governing over northern India – in this way establishing the grounds for the dynasties to come – the Sayyid Dynasty and the Lodi Dynasty.

The Mughal Empire

The Mughal Empire was established by the Mongol leader Babur, in 1526, after he defeated the Ibrahim Lodi, at the first Battle of Panipat. That fight was the very first time when gunpowder was used in India. *Mughal* is the Indo-Aryan version of the word *Mongol*. They retained significant customs of the Mongol culture, and their religion was Islam.

Under the reign of Akbar the Great, the Mughal Empire expanded considerably and consistently, and it continued down this path until the end of Aurangzeb's rule. This was due to more than the military victories he accomplished; the empire under the reign of Akbar is distinguished for the excellent administrative organization and coherent policy – these are the main aspects that sustained the empire for approximately 150 years.

He set the solid grounds for correct provincial administration, by fixing territories of the rural lands and initiating a standard administrative model aiming at meeting local circumstances.

Akbar's son – Jahangir – governed the empire between 1605 and 1627. At the end of his reign, the empire was large and wealthy, being acknowledged as one of the grand empires of the time. The Mughals sponsored technology and art, which means they left a rich heritage of paintings, buildings, and literature. A wonderful part of the heritage they left is their beautiful gardens, known as *Jahan Sara*.

A considerable part of the empire's expansion during that time could be attributed to India's developing commercial and cultural contact with the world. Simply put, the 16th and the 17th centuries institutionalized the establishment and expansion of trading organizations in the subcontinent, primarily due to the high demand for Indian goods abroad.

As a result, the Indian regions were drawn to one another, which equaled a more effective trading network. Also, since India had connections with other countries, innovative ideologies and technologies would upgrade their imperial edifice.

It could be argued that the empire, itself, was a historical experiment. The Mughal culture was blended with Indian and Perso-Islamic regional elements, and the result was unique.

After Aurangzeb's death in 1707, the empire began to decline steadily. Irrespective of that, somehow it managed to preserve part of its influence in the Indian subcontinent for other 150 years.

What Determined the Decline of the Mughal Empire?

A question that imminently emerges is what caused the downfall of the Mughal Empire, considering that it has grown to become so powerful and influential? We'll briefly analyze the aspects that triggered that.

The far-reaching Mughal Empire was beyond being effectively controlled by its rulers. Aurangzeb aimed at expanding the geographical borders of the empire, even though that would cost him the lives of thousands, plus large amounts of money. Apart from that, he denied the Rajputs, Marathas and the Jats regional autonomy, which abolished the preceding autonomy that existed between them and the Mughal Empire.

Another mistake was the fact that he forced the inclusion of a centralized system of governance, in areas that were beyond his control. Simply put, Aurangzeb was unsuccessful at making fruitful alliances to protect his empire. On the contrary, his decision led to him having more and more enemies.

Another noteworthy cause that eventually led to the decline of the empire was the peasant unrest. The rebellion acts of the Jats and Bundelas was primarily due to the exploitation of the peasants.

The growing class of subadars wanted to maximize their profits. Hence, they exploited peasants. On the opposite side, at the Mughal court, there was an obvious display of richness and luxuries. The state of unrest in which the Empire was at that time dramatically affected the commerce and trade.

The condition of the average Indian peasant decreased significantly during the 17th and the 18th centuries. Nobles placed a lot of pressure on the peasants and oppressed them, sometimes by violating official regulations. Consequently, many peasants chose to unite and create roving bands of robberies and adventures. The appearance and growth of such rebellious groups undermined the order and law of the Mughal Empire. It also questioned the efficacy of the governing system.

As for the Mughal Army, it was short of discipline and fighting morale. The unavailability of financing made it challenging to maintain a large army. The officers and soldiers weren't paid accordingly, which led to other complications.

Furthermore, it is also assumed that the crisis of the jagirdari system could have been a cause. What did this system imply? The allocation of a piece of land to a person in order to gather revenue in exchange for cash salary. That was actually an old practice in India. The Mughal Empire implemented this system as well. The areas allocated were referred to as Jagirs, whereas the holders were referred to as Jagirdars. So, what was it that caused the emergence of the crisis? The problem appeared due to a shortage of jagirs and the plethora of jaghirdars.

This issue gave the system an exploitative nature, establishing the ground that would determine the imperial instability.

On the other hand, it could be argued that the governance of the Mughal Empire depended significantly on the effectiveness of the emperor's rule. Simply put, the emperor was conveyed as one of the central pillars of the empire. His capability of keeping decentralizing elements at a distance was primordial in this respect.

The Maratha Empire

The Maratha Empire was established by the renowned warrior known as Chatrapati Shivaji, in 1674, in the proximity of Bijapur. The Marathas became more powerful when the influence of the Mughal Empire started to decline around the 17th century, due to the reasons enumerated above.

Essentially, the Maratha Empire was widely influential from 1674 to 1818. At its very peak, the empire would rule over 250 million acres. They were talented, ambitious warriors, being brutally possessive with their land.

So, how was this empire founded? After a sequence of military battles against Mughal emperor Aurangzeb, Shivaji established the Maratha nation. Irrespective of his success, after his death in 1680, he left the kingdom defenseless to attacks and external aggression. Until 1749, the state of Maratha was governed by Shahu, Shivaji's grandson. During his rule, Shahu appointed a prime minister, or a Peshwa, who was given the right to act as the head of the state if the kingdom struggled with emergencies. In time, the prime ministers earned more rights, and they became the *real* rulers of the state, while Shivaji's successors were merely nominal heads of the empire.

In essence, the Marathas were a Marathi speaking clan. The advance of the Marathas is one of the many reasons that triggered the decline of the Mughal Empire. The rulers that followed after Shivaji managed to keep the empire together, in this way making it one of the strongest empires in India.

The empire would control central India, the Deccan, and some sections of present-day Pakistan. Nevertheless, the empire struggled with hardships at the hands of the Afghans in the third battle of Panipat. Afterward, the British came to India, and they wanted to incorporate the Maratha Empire into the Bombay Presidency. At that time, the size of the empire was dramatically reduced to a regional kingdom.

Notwithstanding, the Marathas were unyielding about their territory and conducted three battles against the British. Eventually, the British ended up annexing the land that was governed by the Peshwas. In this way, the rule of a great empire was ended.

The Maratha Empire had a revolutionary nature. It brought dramatic changes to the Indian society. From the very start, religious pluralism and tolerance stood at the foundation of this reign. These two were the elementary pillars on which the society was established, as Shivaji acknowledged their crucial importance.

Secondly, what made the empire truly unique was the fact that it didn't follow the rules of the caste system. That being said, the priestly class – the Brahmins, were acknowledged as the prime ministers of the warrior class – the Kshatriya. Thirdly, what made this empire grow was the fact that it encompassed a wide range of skilled individuals whose contribution made the society flourish.

Each group was well represented in the empire. Additionally, their military controlled extensive segments of the country. Since they promoted a policy of religious tolerance, they accepted the Hindu interests as well, acting as a significant back-pressure opposing the ever-growing Mughal influence.

Present day's partitioned India accounts for part of the area that belonged to the Maratha Confederacy. Contrary to the Mughal Empire that wasn't interested in building a powerful navy, the Maratha Empire chose otherwise. The legendary Kanhoji Angre was the one that led the fleet when it reached its peak.

The Bhakti Movement and Its Noteworthy Significance

Saints and Sufis were acknowledged as prominent religious gurus in the medieval period. Also, it's worth noting the influence of Bhakti saints, whose teachings were quite powerful during the time.

It could be argued that the Bhakti movement constitutes a prominent chapter in the socio-cultural history of India. Surprisingly enough, the concept of Bhakti wasn't innovative in the Indian tradition – in truth, it is as old as Hinduism.

However, if we were to address the Bhakti movement in the socio-religious Indian context, it would have a distinct connotation. The Bhakti movement represents the society's response to the features linked to the Islamic religion. Put differently; this movement could be perceived as a response to Islam's egalitarianism and monotheism, which determined a reinterpretation of Hinduism.

Substantially, the Bhakti movement started as a reaction against the ritualism, inaccessibility and caste division that featured the Indian society at that time. Devotion represented the primary element in the Bhakti cult, the one that could facilitate the unity of the human soul with God. Although the basic concepts promoted by the Bhakti movement were present in the Vedas, those values weren't practiced by the masses until the movement of the Bhakti saints.

In essence, Bhakti saints and followers didn't conform to any religion, customs or orders. They strongly believed in worshipping one God, and they were utterly devoted to that purpose. They also acknowledged that all men were created equal while condemning image worship, class, and caste distinction. Apart from that, they also denounced useless ceremonies, blind faith and a range of religious practices.

What the Bhakti saints attempted to do is rehabilitate the Brahmanical caste and class divided society by embracing the Islamic concept of one God. According to some scholars, the Bhakti cult was significantly influenced by Islamism and its beliefs. On the other hand, other scholars indicate that the cult brought to the attention the principles presented in the Vedas.

This period witnessed an increase of saints who aimed at reforming Hinduism and eliminating meaningless practices and rituals. Apart from that, the 15th century is acknowledged as being the era of tolerance and harmony in India.

This movement highlighted the need of a Guru or preceptor who would guide the devotees. It was centered on monotheism, and the emphasis was placed on worshipping God in order to accomplish salvation.

One of the changes that took place during this timeframe is

that various immoral actions were frowned upon and discouraged. Another notable impact was that it institutionalized unity between Muslim and Hindu communities, promoting the spirit of tolerance. These teachings aimed at healing the suppressed class, and they had long-lasting effects. This movement laid the grounds for a mixed and liberal Indian society.

Furthermore, the Bhakti movement played a crucial role in revolutionizing the character of Vedic Hinduism. By introducing and highlighting the cult of Bhakti as a means of attaining salvation, Bhagavatism diminished the significance of the ritual of Vedic sacrifices.

It's true that the Vedic rites survived; nevertheless, their popularity was significantly diminished as a result of the growing influence of the Bhakti cult. Bhagavata worshippers were primarily liable for the introduction of the image worship in the context of Brahmanical Hinduism. That being said, the representation of Vishnu gave the start to promoting image worship.

This movement brought to the attention of both Muslims and Hindus that rituals and superstitions were futile. This gave birth to the appreciation of the difference between distinct religions.

On the whole, the Bhakti movement managed to accomplish two important objectives. For starters, it reformed Hinduism, and secondly, it developed a harmonious relationship between the Muslims and Hindus. Additionally, it determined the birth of a new sect, namely Sikhism.

Apart from that, the Bhakti movement had a notable influence on Indian rulers, who started to treat their subjects generously, impartially and equally. National rulers, such as Abkbar, who encouraged a national way of thinking, were especially influenced by this movement.

The Effects of the Bhakti Movement on the Medieval Indian Society

In order to fully grasp the impact of the Bhakti movement, we should have a look at the background when this cultural movement gained momentum. Since the Hindus were under Muslim rule, they had experienced a lot of hardships: material, spiritual and moral. Muslim rulers aimed at enforcing the Islamic laws and way of thinking on the Hindus, which had a harmful effect on the society.

In this respect, the Bhakti movement wanted to bring support and hope. Apart from that, in time, various evil practices had been implemented into the Hindu society, the most notable being the class distinction, which determined the division of the community.

In the meantime, among the foreign invaders, there were the Sufi Muslims that had a liberal way of thinking. They outlined the importance of virtues such as devotion, brotherhood, love, and equality. It is needless to say that this contributed to harmonizing the conflicting interests, bringing Muslims and Hindus closer.

A noteworthy element that triggered the growing popularity of the Bhakti movement was that the promoters highlighted that Rahim and Rama were the same. Apart from that, they also condemned the hatred that has divided the society into halves.

The Hindus acknowledged that it was challenging, if not impossible to drive away the Muslims from India. On the opposite side, the Muslims recognized that the Hindus were a majority, and imposing their Islamist beliefs was an unattainable goal. So, in the social context of the Bhakti movement, both sides aimed at making efforts to get over their differences. The Sufi saints acted on behalf of the Muslims while the Hindu saints acted in the name of the Hindus.

Both Muslim and Hindu saints emphasized the religious

simplicity, moral attitudes, and human qualities. They outlined that a genuinely religious man is the one whose actions and thoughts are pure.

Common Misconceptions about Medieval India

1. Indians Didn't Have Access to Medical Care

Presumably, when one thinks about medieval time, he/she assumes that, during that period, people didn't have access to state-of-the-art medical care. Truth be told, medical knowledge in India had quite an early start. Even in the Stone Age, around 5000 BC, there were dentists at Mehrgahr, namely in the Hindus River Valley (present-day Pakistan), who would fix people's cavities.

Shushruta was one of the first peoples in history that studied the human anatomy. In fact, he described in detail the anatomy by using a dead body. Apart from that, he was skillful in plastic surgeries; his greatest contribution is thought to be the operation of rhinoplasty – which refers to the restoration of a mutilated nose.

In 1000 BC, doctors from northern India wrote a comprehensive medical textbook – the *Atharva Veda,* which focused on explaining various treatments for diseases. Notwithstanding, similar to Egyptian medical texts originating from the same period, this textbook indicated that diseases are mainly caused by bad spirits, so they had to be killed with spells or poisons.

Nevertheless, by 200 AD, Indian doctors relinquished the idea that bad spirits caused illnesses. Doctor Charaka reckoned that prevention was the best solution for numerous diseases, which is why he suggested keeping the rumors in balance in order to stay healthy. Indian doctors were extremely respected at that time. As a result, they would sell their medicine to people from Iran, the Roman Empire, China, East Africa, and so on.

Hundreds of years later, Indian doctors were the first that came up with a cure to inoculate people against smallpox. After the Islamic invasion, many Iranian doctors came to India. They brought henbane and opium. By the 1200s AD, Indian doctors knew that opium could be used as an anesthetic.

2. Muslim Rulers Didn't Destroy Thousands of Hindu Temples and Universities

At the moment, there is an ongoing debate regarding the *actual* destruction of temples and universities by the Muslim invaders in medieval India. Nevertheless, numerous Islamic literary sources offer far-reaching evidence regarding the destruction of temples.

The area that used to be the cradle where the Hindu culture evolved was filled with ruins of what used to be magnificent monasteries and temples belonging to schools of Buddha, Vaishnava, Jaina, Sakta, and so on.

Apart from that, archeological explorations from modern times have demonstrated that most mazars, mosques, zirats that were built on the Indian territory were constructed instead of the Hindu temples and monasteries. What is more, they used the materials from the demolished monuments for finishing their constructions.

Also, numerous Muslim historians from India have described in detail what their heroes did in this respect. Literary evidence highlights one thing: Muslim rulers ravaged Hindu temples on many occasions.

That's because the greater majority of Hindu temples can be found in southern India, or on the eastern coast. For most of their history, these areas were off limits for Muslim rulers. Some of the most devastating destructions took place during the invasion of Mahmud of Ghazni, who came from Afghanistan. In lines with the writings of Persian historians,

Mahmud shattered the prosperity of Hindustan.

Interesting Facts!
- Bhaskaracharya (1114 AD – 1185 AD) was an eminent mathematician, who was renowned as a genius in his time, particularly in geometry and algebra. He was the one who has demonstrated Pythagoras's theorem in merely two lines. He has important works about the gravitational forces, as well.
- Brahmadeva was another academician who lived in Medieval India. His commentaries focused on trigonometry and the way it is linked to astronomy.
-

If It Were Your Choice
Do you agree with Shahu's choice of appointing a prime minister during the Maratha Empire? Would you have done the same or would you have preserved the entire power for yourself? Think about it!

Pop Quiz!
Here are some questions to check your knowledge! If anything, you could always go back to the text and reassess the answers.

1. What are some of the most notable aspects regarding the Chola Dynasty and their rule? How did it impact the Indian culture?
2. Which are the main dynasties that ruled during the Delhi Sultanates?
3. What are the main elements that determined the development of the Mughal Empire?

4. What are the main socio-cultural consequences of the Bhakti movement?

Chapter 3 - British Colonization + East India Company

One of the fundamental reasons why the Europeans would sail the oceans was for finding new trade routes to Asia, India in particular. Apart from the obvious monetary prospect, another important motivation behind the European colonization in distinct parts of the world is often overlooked. It is the deep-rooted belief of *Western supremacy*.

This ideology is also known as *the white man's burden.* In plain English, this is a self-proclaimed mission of the West to bring civilization to any population that doesn't fit the category *west*.

That being said, the Europeans who first came to India had these two intentions in mind. Still, it was the British whose success was notable. Not only that they managed to control a large part of the Indian Territory, but they also aimed at colonizing aspects of the Indian society including culture, education, economy, and politics.

During the 16th and 17th centuries, the British weren't in a good place, from a financial point of view. On the opposite side, India was acknowledged as the richest country at the early time of the 2nd millennia. Apart from that, as we mentioned in the previous chapter, India was one of the first trading nations in the 18th century, holding a monopoly in furnishing first-class spices and textiles. In fact, China and India provided more than half of the world's total trade.

At the beginning of the 18th century, England was coping with economic challenges, due to the Industrial Revolution. This change brought notable improvements; however, the need for capital was greater than ever. In this respect, a considerable amount of the capital investments necessary for the revolution was furnished by India. Surprisingly, India didn't benefit from it in any way.

The British entered the Indian Territory as traders, and their main purpose was to boost their profits by carrying on with the trade. They increased their power gradually as the Mughals and other local rulers gave them permission to expand their trading activities.

As the Mughal Empire showed signs of decline, being fragmented into successor states, the British East India Company presented signs of becoming a political power. The British East India Company realized that in order to earn that power, it had to eradicate other European companies and their trading activities. What they did was to obtain permission for building forts and boosting their military power.

Furthermore, the British had the interest to initiate their monopoly of commerce and trade and continued the process of expanding their political strength in Bengal through the battle of Plassey (1757) and Buxar (1765).

From that point onward, the British East India Company embraced a threefold strategy of military, ideological and colonial administrative measures that would further expand and establish the British Indian Empire.

During this process, we can note an upgrade from trading connections to colonial relations. Through wars, administrative measures, and diplomacy, the British East India Company aimed at maximizing their economic benefits as they fleeced the Indian artisans, farmers, and traders. The process is known as colonization.

The Effects of the British Colonization

The colonialism made India turn into a de-industrialized power. The pattern of colonization witnessed different stages of progress. The Charter Act of 1813, for instance, institutionalized by the British Parliament and Crown nullified the monopoly of the British East India Company. This action opened the gates of commerce and trade for every English citizen.

What is more, according to the Charter Act of 1833, the Governor General of Bengal received the position of Governor General of India, having control over the presidencies of Madras and Bombay.

Apart from that, British citizens were given the permission to own property in India, which raised the number of British landlords and planters of coffee, tea, cotton, and others. In addition, British capitalists embraced other measures such as investing surplus capital in Colonial India. These measures accelerated the process of draining India's wealth.

In addition to the colonialist measures, the British implemented ideologies of orientalism, mercantilism, evangelicalism, liberalism, and utilitarianism to legitimize their colonialist policies in the Indian Territory. In this respect, they tried to brainwash the Indians and the world that what they did was in the interest of development and progress. Apart from that, they claimed that it was *the white man's burden* to *civilize India* from the barbarian rule.

English Education – A Mechanism for Mental Subjugation

The British indicated that an effective way of manipulating the minds of the Indians was by introducing the English education. The native education system was eliminated. Instead, the focus was placed on teaching the Indians about European western art, literature, and languages, in order to separate Indians from their own traditions and culture.

The primary purpose of the British was to create a class of individuals in India that would be British in intellect, opinions, tastes, and morals, even though they would be Indian in color and blood. In other words, the Indian culture and everything it represents was seen as useless and primitive, and the British declared that a whole library of Eastern literature equals a shelf of English literature.

It was argued that the Indians lived in sheer barbarity, and the only cure for that was abolishing their Indian roots.

In this respect, the British introduced a variety of seminars that would educate the Indian Youth in English and Western literature. Even though these institutions enhanced the knowledge of the Indians, they also alienated them from their culture and indigenous knowledge systems. Hence, English values were systematically promoted and forced, in this way replacing India's education system.

What is more, the Governor General of India decided in 1835 that no support was to be provided to students and teachers that pursued native languages and subjects. Moreover, it was further established that all the funds directed towards education would be spent for promoting only English education.

The results of these efforts were noticeable as soon as 1838. The youth trained at Hindu colleges was considerably influenced by English education. In fact, the effects were so notable that a considerable number of the Hindu youngsters originating from noble families no longer agreed with the restrictions of Hinduism, disregarding their rituals and ceremonies. This was the first indication of self-alienation: the Indian people developed a sense of hostility towards their identities.

The British aimed at rewriting India's history and altering its educational system. They used whichever tool they could to demoralize the natives and undermine the cultural significance and authenticity of India.

Considering that the greater majority of Indian leaders were part of the British educational system, this had negatively influenced their psyche and national confidence. Thus, most leaders developed a notable inferiority complex, assuming that if they didn't follow the Western lifestyle, India couldn't flourish.

Christianization – Another Tool of Westernization

Another means through which the British aimed at *westernizing* the Indians was Christianization. That's because they thought that Hinduism, the religion that was prevalent in India, prevented them from exercising ultimate power.

The Scottish missionary Alexander Duff assumed that the Indian philosophy included only foolish, wicked and vain conceptions. It is needless to say that he wasn't the only one who had this opinion on the matter.

In this context, when the East India Company started to increase its control over India, thinkers such as Burke and Edmund highlighted that the company has to *embrace* its moral responsibilities, as well. This implied substituting the Hindu consciousness with the western point of view on religion.

On the whole, we could say that the British had a singular goal in mind: to westernize and promote Christianity in India, using whatever means they could. Although the British weren't the first ones that ruled over India, there is a major distinction between them and the Islamic invaders.

It's true that the Islamic invaders caused destruction, physical damage, and violence, making the Hindus second-class citizens. Still, the British aimed at enslaving the Indian mind and culture on the whole. The British could be held responsible for the physical deprivation and mental self-alienation of the Indians, which didn't end right away. At the time when the British came to India, the country was weakened due to the Islamic forces that determined a sequence of violent battles and wars that harmed the country.

Misconceptions Regarding the British Colonization in India

1. India Benefited from Great Britain's Investment in the Rail System

Most advocates of the colonization indicate that the construction of the Indian Railway System was something India benefited from greatly. Nevertheless, this affirmation is a bit forced, especially if we were to consider the fact that numerous countries built state-of-the-art railway systems without experiencing colonization. That is not all, though: the reality is even more incriminating for the Brits.

Even though the East India Company constructed the railways, they did that for their own benefit, just like everything else. In 1843, Governor-General Lord Hardinge indicated that building the railway could be advantageous to the military, governmental and commercial control of the country.

So, the mere act of constructing the Indian railway was a colonial scam. British shareholders took advantage of that by investing in the railways and attaining great wealth. That's because the government promised investors that their returns would be double.

The government stocks were paid exclusively from Indian taxes. So, in essence, this was a unique source of earnings for the Brits, at the expense of the Indian taxpayers.

What is more, the railways were meant primarily to transport extracted resources such as iron ore, coal, cotton and many others, to Great Britain, where they were manufactured. As for the fact that the railway system facilitated the transportation of the people, this was purely incidental. The third-class compartments, which weren't equipped with necessary amenities, were a source of horror even at that time.

Thereupon, the construction of the Indian Railways was made primarily for the benefit of the Brits. In other words, the installation of the railway system solved the problem of transporting British goods to India, where it sold them. And secondly, British shareholders made massive amounts of cash by investing in the railways, as the government promised fantastic returns on capital, all paid from Indian taxes.

2. Great Britain Turned India into the Country It Is Today

Another common misconception is that the colonial rule in India facilitated the development of present-day India. Many people convey India as a developing country that wouldn't have made it if it weren't for the colonization period. That is far from being true.

The colonial rule equaled economic exploitation, at its finest. It destroyed thriving industries; it eliminated indigenous institutions of governance.

In 1600, when the East India Company was first set up, Britain produced only 1.8 percent of the world's GDP. On the other hand, India produced approximately 23 percent, 27 percent by 1700. Furthermore, by 1940, at the end of the British rule, Great Britain generated 10 percent of the world's GDP, while India was acknowledged as a poor, third-world country, which was coping with starvation. When the British left from India, the life expectancy in India was of 27, the percentage of literacy was 16 percent, and there wasn't a domestic industry. 90 percent of the Indians were below the acceptable poverty line.

Simply put, when the British first reached India, the country was a wealthy, commercializing and thriving country. In fact, that is the primary reason the Brits have shown interest in colonizing it. It was far from being underdeveloped since pre-colonial India would export first-class quality goods. The British elite was keen on wearing Indian silk and linen, and they used their spices in the cuisine.

Interesting Facts!

- Britain's Industrial Revolution was actually developed because the Indian cloth production was de-industrialized. Indians were enforced to import British products. This way, they facilitated their revolution.
- During Great Britain's ruthless exploitation of India, between 15 and 29 million Indians died tragically due to starvation and malnutrition.
- Approximately four million Bengalis died in 1943, during the Great Bengal Famine after Winston Churchill knowingly ordered the diversion of food from Indians civilians to European stockpiles and British soldiers.
- India contributed with more soldiers to the British Army during World War One than New Zealand, South Africa, Canada and Australia combined.
- The cost of the British Army was funded from revenues that originated from India. The average sum per year was estimated at 19,000,000 pounds.

If It Were Your Choice

What would you have done if you were a British soldier living in India during the time of the Colonization? Would you have acted the same as most English newcomers, assuming you were entitled to behave in that way?

Pop Quiz!

1. What was the political and economic context in Britain at the beginning of the 18th century?
2. Which are the main battles that highlighted the supremacy of the British on Indian Land?
3. What facilitated the coming of the British? What was the economic context in India?
4. What ideologies did the British use to brainwash the Indian society?
5. What was the effect of introducing the British education system in India?

Chapter 4 - India from 1949 until the Present

In the previous chapter, we briefly analyzed the way in which the British colonization impacted the Indians and the way in which their taxations impoverished the society. Apart from that, they aimed at denying them their national identity, civilization, and history.

In this respect, the struggle for independence was a movement initiated for breaking free from subjugations. The independence movement incorporated a range of strategies from revolutionary acts of violence, to non-violent, peaceful protests. Officially, India attained its independence on August 15th, 1947.

What are the main aspects that facilitated this, and what role did each play?

For starters, the spirit of nationalism in India started to spread in the middle of the 19th century, which was further empowered by the establishment of the Indian National Congress in 1885. The indifferent and authoritative attitude of the British towards Indian sentiments contributed to the national movement.

National leaders whose names are well-known, such as Mahatma Gandhi, Vallabhai Patel, Pandit Jawaharlal Nehru, Netaji Subhash Bose and many others, have united their strengths and fought for the administrative and political rights of the people. In this context, the British have embraced a plan of implementing division between the Muslims and Hindus, which lead to the formation of the Muslim League.

The outburst of World War Two temporarily shelved the Indian issue. The British asked for the help of the Indians in battle, which boosted the Indian National Congress' power. This was of crucial importance since Britain was weak as it has lost a lot of men during World War One. In exchange, Mahatma Gandhi asked for independence – because of this, the British put the entire Indian National Congress in jail.

Irrespective of that, Indian soldiers still fought for Britain; however, other Indians, such as Netaji Subhash Bose chose to support Nazi Germany and Japan. As the war ended, Britain was weakened, while India's fighting skills have enhanced. Even though Britain aimed at controlling India and it's wealth by making promises, the numbers of Indians that participated in the non-violent demonstrations led by Gandhi placed an end to the dreaded taxes and the British rule.

On that note, in 1947, the Indian National Congress finalized the negotiations for India's independence from Britain. Nevertheless, Britain wanted to divide the land into two separate countries, according to their religious practices. So, Pakistan would be an Islamic state whereas India would be a Hindu country. Although Gandhi kept on fighting to reunite India and Pakistan into one country, he was shot in 1948. Millions of Indians were forced to move to the *right* country depending on their religion, many being killed in the riots that made them move.

That leads us to a logical question: what direction did India take after the *transfer of power?* To begin with, the creation of the Constitution of India was of primary importance. This created a roadmap for the country's future.

India earned its independence with the condition that the country would be parted. As we already indicated, a new state of Pakistan was established, and considerable portions of Eastern and Western India were taken away from the Indian map. To be more precise, West Pakistan took away Sindh, Western Punjab, and Baluchistan while East Pakistan was established with the partition of Bengal into West and East. Hence, East Pakistan and West Pakistan were separated by the Indian Territory.

In 1971, East Pakistan became a separate country – namely Bangladesh. So, the subcontinent was separated into three different nations.

That being said, independence was introduced in India along with a mixture of legacies and heritages. Furthermore, the partitions led to the dislocation of populations on both sides. Many Hindu families moved to India as refugees or Muslim families that moved to Pakistan.

These movements caused a lot of unrest, bloodshed, looting, merciless murders, rape, and other similar things.

On that note, the transition from a colonial country to an independent one wasn't easy. The partition led to the division of resources, the reorientation of bureaucracy, and the transfer of government personnel from a country to another.

It could be argued that the events that followed represented the other stages India had to take towards development. The new constitution, which was implemented on the 26th of November 1949 by the Constituent Assembly aided India to part from their British colonial past.

The Constitution included a chapter on Fundamental Rights and Directive Principles. The addition of adult suffrage was a novelty, as well. Thus, India's policy would become a combination of federal and unitary forms of government. The new leadership was eager to implement socio-economic reforms.

Additionally, the Indian constitution also challenged Indians to rise above religious differences, while safeguarding the country's *composite culture* that makes it so unique in its diversity.

Jawaharlal Nehru as Prime Minister

Jawaharlal Nehru was a prominent figure in the political

context after India has gained its independence. He was referred to as *Pandit Nehru,* as pandit meant wise man. Additionally, he was the primary architect of both foreign and domestic politics during 1947 and 1964. He was born into a wealthy family, and he received proper education at Cambridge. From a political mindset, he incorporated a fusion of ideas: he was an ardent nationalist, a pragmatic socialist, and secular when it came to religion. His personal charisma, breadth of vision and intellect made him widely popular throughout India; hence, he was reelected in the elections from 1952, 1957, and 1962.

In his early political career, Nehru was Gandhi's disciple. He was a part of the Indian National Congress Party, becoming its leader in 1929. Consequently, several times, he was arrested. His priority was to grow the number of supporters of the Indian independence. Hence, he would travel around the country to spread the word.

The pillars that stood at the foundation of Nehru's rule were the following: socialism, democracy, secularism, and alignment. Being the leader of democratic India, he aimed at combining the principles of Fabian socialism with parliamentary democracy. Historians indicated that he had strong democratic instincts and a sense of propriety that was typical of the English people.

At the London School of Economics, he learned the Fabian notions of socialism. He attempted to put into practice the notions he gained during his studies. He managed to create a country that was democratic, secular and republican, featuring a powerful centralized state that defined the nation and facilitated its economic development. Nehru was aware of the state of poverty India was struggling with, at that time. Hence, by 1951, he created a program to build *temples of modern India:* roads, power plants, dams, and so on.

Two Economic Phases

Independent India dealt with a shattered economy, shocking poverty, and widespread illiteracy. Its economic growth is separated into two distinct phases: 45 years after the independence and two decades of free market economy. The years that followed immediately after the independence were featured by instances in which economic development was stopped due to unsuitable policies.

What rescued India was the introduction of economic reforms with the institutionalization of a policy of privatization and liberalization. The main aspects that favored India's economic growth were the economic reforms of 1991, increased FDI, a boosted domestic consumption and the adoption of information technology.

The Development of the Agriculture Sector

Starting from the 1950s, steady progress has been noted in the agriculture sector. In truth, it developed by 1 percent per year in the first half of the 20th century. What is more, after the post-independence era, the rate of growth reached 2.6 percent. Introducing high-yielding varieties of crops and expanding the farming areas were the two main elements that facilitated the expansion of the agricultural production.

Considerable and consistent investments in land reforms, research, and enhancement of rural infrastructure were the factors that promoted the existence of an agricultural revolution in India. Apart from that, the country developed in the agri-biotech sector as well, which has been developing at a rate of 30 percent in the last years.

Scientific Accomplishments

Independent India has embraced a range of ambitious projects, such as the launch of their first satellite, namely

Aryabhatta in 1975. From that point onward, India had launched other successful satellites, starting their first mission to Mars in 2013. India aims at developing missile and nuclear programs, and it is renowned as an independent force in this field.

Breakthroughs in the Education System

As we already mentioned, after the declaration of independence, India was coping with widespread illiteracy. Still, it managed to bring its educational system at global standards.

During the post-independence era, a considerable number of schools were built. The Parliament decided that elementary education would be one of the children's fundamental rights, by including the 86th amendment to the Constitution in 2002. During the independence, the rate of literacy in India was 12.2 percent, which grew by 74.4 percent in 2011.

Furthermore, the government inaugurated the Sarva Siksha Abhiyan in 2001, to provide education to all children between 6 and 14 years.

Infrastructure Development

At the moment, the Indian road network is acknowledged as the largest in the world. The total length has grown from 0.399 million km in 1951 to 4.24 million km in 2014. What is more, the length of the country's national highways increased from 24,000 km (1947-1969) to 92,851 km (2014). These governmental actions have led to industrial growth, which further facilitated the development of the country.

Apart from that, India embraced a multi-pronged approach to energy. After about seven decades of independence, India is renowned as the third most important producer of electricity in Asia.

Common Misconceptions

1. India Should be Grateful for Colonialism

The most damaging long-term action of Great Britain on India was, presumably, the partition of India into three countries: India, Pakistan and (eventually) Bangladesh. From that point onward, the relationships between these countries have become worse and worse.

This partition determined one of the most important migrations in history. It displaced approximately 15 million people, determining the deaths of many.

2. Britain's Influence on India Ended after Colonization

Great Britain considered itself as being an eminent ally of the region; hence, it continued meddling in Indian politics. The most notable example is what happened in 1984 when the British government suggested the Indian government to consider the Operation Blue Star – one of the most catastrophic battles in military history. Consequently, this operation led to the raiding of the Golden Temple, a holy sanctuary for Sikhs, determining the deaths of hundreds.

After this followed Gandhi's assassination and other subsequent attacks against the Sikh population of India. That contributed to the deaths of over 2,000 Sikhs in Delhi. Nevertheless, Britain admitted playing a role in this only a couple of years ago.

3. India Is a Rich Country

Although India is continually developing, and it has made remarkable progress after gaining its independence, this didn't eradicate poverty. Paradoxically, according to official reports, India is acknowledged as one of the 10 ten richest countries in the world, with a total individual wealth of $5,200 billion. On the other side, by calculating that considering the capita basis, one could determine that the average Indian is *quite poor*.

India's official poverty rate is 22 percent. Nevertheless, these statistics refer exclusively to the Indians that live in abject scenarios. On the opposite, 56 percent of Indians lack the ways to meet their fundamental means. While food is considered among the primary concerns for the poor, sanitation, and health care pose other problems, as well. On the whole, Indians don't have access to half the health care and infrastructure they would need.

While it's true that India has made extraordinary gains against acute poverty, the reality is that approximately 680 million Indian citizens have to live with distinct forms of deprivation.

The contradiction of terms is still there. India wants to develop into a superpower, and it has all the means to accomplish that, but a considerable part of the population still struggles with poverty. Its economic growth has created two distinct societies: one poor and the other rich.

Interesting Facts!
- It is believed that Mahatma Gandhi was the creator of the Indian Flag, but, in fact, it was Pingali Venkavya – one of the most important figures that fought for Indian freedom – that created the flag.
- In March 1930, Gandhi, the figure that would later become known as the father of the Indian nation, marched a protest against Great Britain's rule. He marched from the western Indian city of Ahmedabad to Gujarat, for a distance of 250 miles.

If It Were Your Choice
What would you have done if you were in Jawaharlal Nehru's

shoes? What actions would you have taken in order to facilitate India's development and *rise from the ashes,* after the struggle it has gone through before the independence?

Pop Quiz!

1. When did India proclaim its independence? What conditions did the British impose on them?
2. What makes 1949 an important year in India's history?
3. What struggles did India cope with after the proclamation of independence?
4. What facilitated India's economic growth and what are the main areas where most improvements are noted?

Chapter 5 - Indian Politics and Its Role in the World Today

India's population is one billion. This makes it the second most heavily populated country in the entire world. Apart from that, this would mean that every sixth person in the world is Indian. It holds the title for being the largest democracy in the world, and their political system includes a mixture of features, flaws included. What is more, their democratic system differentiates itself greatly from other democratic attempts such as Bangladesh and Pakistan, which were part of India until 1947.

Distinct from the British or American political systems, which have remained unaltered for years, the Indian political system has been established more recently.

The Effects of the Indian Partition

India's first experience with democracy started on the 15th of August when the British gave up on their political power over India. After attaining political independence at the cost of dividing one country in two, the Indians experienced the aching tragedy of the division. The trauma of this division lingers in the hearts of the people living in India, Bangladesh, and Pakistan.

The inexcusable political division due to religion differences has led to four full- fledged wars between Pakistan and India, a division of Pakistan, land grabs, terrorism, and others. The independent country that was born in 1947 still struggles to find its identity.

The Indian Constitution

The present constitution came into being on the 26th of January 1950, and it supports the trinity of equality, liberty, and justice for its citizens. In truth, the Indian constitution is acknowledged as the longest in the world, containing 444 articles, 98 amendments, 12 schedules – the version in English has about 120,000 words.

Apart from that, the Indian constitution has implemented approximately 100 changes, making it the most amended national documents in the world. Many of these changes have taken place after long-lasting disputes between the Supreme Court and the Parliament, most of them being related to the rights of the parliamentary sovereignty.

In spite of the attempts of overturning its emancipatory visions, the constitution remains a document and a vision that promises to promote justice, equality and opportunity.

The Executive Branch

The president is the head of the Indian state. Typically, this could be conveyed as a ceremonial role, originally shaped after the British monarch's role of advising, encouraging and warning the government when it comes to constitutional matters. On that note, if it's necessary, the president can choose to return a Parliamentary Bill for reconsideration, in the event of a crisis. Furthermore, the president could declare a state of emergency, which would make it possible to expand the presidency period.

Approximately 4,500 members belonging to the national parliament and state legislators are qualified to vote when it comes to president elections. At the moment, Pranab Mukherjee is president in India.

As for the Vice President, he is also chosen by the members of an electoral college encompassing both houses of parliament. The prime minister is recognized as the head of the government, and he is typically appointed by the president. Nadendra Modi became prime minister in May 2014, although until then he didn't hold a political position.

The Legislative Branch

The Indian political system incorporates *the lower house,* which is referred to as Lok Sabha – the House of the People. As it is established in the constitution, the maximum number of members is 552, including 530 members that stand for each Indian state, 20 members that represent the people from the Union Territories and two members that stand for the Anglo-Indian community. At the moment, the house consists of 545 members.

Each Lok Sabha is established for a five-year timeframe. Afterward, it automatically dissolves. The only exception is in the case of a Proclamation of Emergency that would extend the term. This has happened three times until now.

As for the upper house, it is named Rajya Sabha, or the Council of States. The Constitution indicates that it should have up to 250 members. The president chooses 12 members with expertise in specific fields of literature, art, social services, and science. The single transferable vote is the method of election in local legislatures.

The two houses administer the legislative power, apart from the area of supplying money. In this situation, the Lok Sabha have widespread influence. In the event of inaccurate legislation, a sitting is held. If the problem isn't solved this way, a joint session of the Parliament is held.

Corruption

Distinct from other democracies based in Europe and America, India struggles with corruption on a greater level. Incidents such as the assassination of the highly-acknowledged Mahatma Gandhi in 1948 and the assassination of Prime Minister Indira Gandhi and Prime Minister Rajiv Gandhi indicate that.

Caste, regional and communal tensions still haunt Indian

politics. At times, these tensions even jeopardize the long-standing secular and democratic ethos.

In the recent years, the emergence of RTI activists has been noted: thousands of citizens, often coping with poverty, sometimes even illiteracy utilize the Right To Information legislation of 2005 to advocate transparency and battle corruption in public institutions. In the first five years after this legislation was introduced, approximately 1 million RTI requests have been filed, thus threatening the authority.

On the whole, corruption isn't new to India, as it is a fundamental element featuring the Indian society. The severity of the corruption ranges from small, rather insignificant police bribes to macro scale, election-influencing actions. That being said, protests against corruption represent a common sight in India. They usually result in the political class' promises that it will be eradicated in the foreseeable future.

Nevertheless, the root of corruption is much more complex than it appears. When the British first came to India, they recognized that due to the notable discretionary powers of the administrators, they could be tempted to embrace corruption. As a result, they initiated a system that ensured the British officials were well-paid, and that severely punished signs of dishonesty.

In 1947, when India gained its independence, Prime Minister Nehru preserved the wide-reaching powers of the British colonial administration, including laws that entitled officials to interfere in almost every aspect of daily life. Concurrently, he also significantly diminished the salaries in the public sector.

These decisions created a system in which a considerable number of poorly paid public employees had the opportunity of *maximizing their earnings* through governmental coercion. Hence, from that point onward, corruption spread in the public system.

For example, the average policeman in India has such a poor salary that accepting bribery is almost part of the wage structure. Based on official data, in 2009, the housing allowance for the head of the police department in Mumbai, which is one of the most expensive cities in the entire world, was $45 per month. Thus, to afford to make a living, one is likely to accept bribery. Typically, the *income supplement* refers to minor cases, such as a small pay off at a traffic stop. Notwithstanding, once this becomes normality, it can spread deep and fast.

Secondly, the taxation system is another source of problems. By the 1970s, the ones who earned the most had to pay 93.5 percent in tax. In some situations, the combined wealth and income taxes could end up exceeding the actual income. That being said, it was literally impossible to survive considering that one paid those taxes.

Concurrently, a variety of profitable sectors were overly controlled by the government, including foreign trade and the sale of liquor. Consequently, in the 1960s, similar to what happened in the United Stated during the prohibition, mafia gained ultimate control of these sectors, generating massive amounts of black profit.

Apart from that, politicians are also paid very poorly. Thus, since they are likely to remain in office for four years only, they maximize the time they spend in this position to secure their family's future by setting up connections that would either ensure they get re-elected or that they get well out of the office. Apart from that, they are also prone to take advantage of their positions to generate cash and get involved in fishy businesses.

Considering these primary elements (and many others), nowadays, India is caught in a situation in which most of its sectors are affected by epidemic corruption. In this direction, it is estimated that approximately $1.4 trillion is the amount of Indian black money present in offshore accounts. What is more, according to a recent survey conducted by Transparency International – an anti-corruption global society organization – India has the highest rate of bribery in Asia. Seven out of ten people had paid a bribe when they accessed public services in India.

Indian Politics and Its Role in the World

At the moment, India is getting involved in world politics by participating in international organizational meetings. India aims at making friendly connections with almost every country. Considering that India is the most fast-growing economy in the entire world, numerous companies wish to invest in this country.

Furthermore, India aims at obtaining a permanent position in the United Nations by getting the support of members. Apart from that, India has trilateral, bilateral and strategic treaties with USA, Japan, Russia, Australia and others regarding economic development, terrorism, technological development, space technology, social development, defense and nuclear technology.

That being said, India is a prominent member of WTO, IMF, and East Asia Summit, etc. India is considered to be a crucial economic player, which is the primary reason why most countries in the world want to maintain positive relationships. The focus is placed on economics and geopolitics, much more than it used to be in the past.

Nonetheless, for this global presence to be more prominent, their political system has to be revamped, embracing an approach that would address the needs of the population. However, India's strategic capabilities and commitment to enhancing its regional and global influence shouldn't be overlooked.

Being one of the giants of the developing world, India has

great responsibilities. Ultimately, the question that follows is: *how well can it administer its notable advantages in a manner that will maximize its future security while promoting economic growth?*

Misconceptions about Indian Politics

1. Corruption Is the Only Aspect that Holds India Back

It's 100 percent accurate that corruption is a pregnant concern in the Indian socio-political context. Nevertheless, to say that this is the only problem is a bit naive. According to official information, two-thirds of the Indian population work as farmers. Irrespective of that, they account for only 1/5 of GDP (gross domestic product). As a result, they cope with poverty, and they don't have the opportunity to surpass their condition.

One the primary causes of this noteworthy discrepancy is that farmers experience trade barriers, such as the *Agricultural Produce Market Committee (APMC)*. This restricts farmers in terms of whom they are allowed to sell their produce. Nevertheless, these problems aren't addressed.

That being said, if growth would be a priority, the agricultural economy should be changed, hence liberalized, which would enable farmers to sell freely. When rural industries and farmers will have access to a regular income, they will be more likely to make investments, which will enhance their productivity. That, in exchange, will set the grounds for economic equality.

Secondly, another reason why India isn't as developed as it *could be* is the fact that it doesn't invest in innovation as much as it should. It goes without saying that India doesn't lack leading minds that could create first-class products that would address the needs and requirements of the market. In this respect, India should decide between playing the role of an important power that serves multinationals by supplying software engineers or becoming a lead player in this context.

Apart from that, if India would implement technology in its educational system, things could change dramatically. At the moment, the Indian educational system copes with a notable shortage of adequately prepared teachers. What's more, out of 630,000 villages in India, more than 500,000 aren't equipped with schools that provide education above seventh grade.

2. Mahatma Gandhi Is Responsible for the Indian Partition

The Indian partition is an event in Indian history that is attributed to numerous individuals. Some consider that Mahatma Gandhi is one of the men that could be held liable for this unfortunate turn of events, others say that it was Mohammed Ali Jinnah, while others indicate it was Jawaharlal Nehru/Sardar Patel. The list of speculations could go on forever. It's true that there were distinct situations in which each of these persons supported one cause or another. Nevertheless, affirming that this could make them liable for the partition would be an exaggeration.

Before the arrival of the British on the Indian Territory, the Muslims were the official rulers of the country. The people that occupied important positions were Muslims, as for the court language, it was Persian until 1842. Nevertheless, with the coming of the British, their status had been significantly reduced, and they were the equals of their Hindu fellow-countrymen.

By the 1890s, Bengal was acknowledged as one of the most attractive regions in India, which posed a lot of problems to the British rule. In this context, both the Muslim and the Hindu fought against the British. In order to weaken their power, Curzon separated Bengal into East Bengal and West Bengal. Once again, the *divide and conquer* principle is applied. East Bengal was largely populated by Muslims while West Bengal was vastly populated by Hindus. Consequently, this determined the formation of the Muslim League, which is actually among the driving forces that facilitated the partition of India.

Secondly, the GOI Act 1909 is another excellent example of the same principle: *divide and conquer*. It promoted a separate electorate for Muslims. It is needless to say that this action has made a long-lasting separation between the Muslims and Indians. Gradually, this resulted in the demand for establishing a separate, individual state.

At first, when this affirmation was made, it wasn't taken seriously. Nevertheless, eventually, this concept gained popularity especially in the Northwestern part of the Indian continent. The Muslim minority assumed that they weren't rightfully presented in leadership roles – Indian Police, Civil Services, so on. For the most part, these assumptions weren't accurate; but they were exploited by their leaders in order to further divide the nation.

In the 1940s, the Muslim League brought into discussion the dual nation theory. According to this theory, religion is the fundamental element that should define the nationality of a country. This ideology was widely used by Muhammad Ali Jinnah. He referred to it as being the *awakening of the Muslims for establishing Pakistan*. The two-nation theory was fathered by Sir Syed Ahmed Khan.

The effects of this partition were paramount as it resulted in communal riots at Punjab and other military violent conflicts. These conflicts made the partition inevitable.

I'll summarize once again the main elements that laid the grounds for the partition. Firstly, the British had implanted seeds of distrust in Hindu and Muslim population. These were fructified by the politicians of the All India Muslim League. Apart from that, a general sense of discontent among the Muslims created the perfect background that would give the start to the numerous riots that took place before the Independence.

Interesting Facts!

- Mahatma Gandhi received five distinct nominations for the Nobel Peace Prize.
- India is acknowledged as a notable regional power due to its economic growth, size, and population. Typically, it has focused on diplomacy, as opposed to relying on its might.

If It Were Your Choice

Place yourself in Gandhi's shoes: what would you have done to maximize your country's chances of gaining independence? Would you have been as peaceful as he was in his attempt, or would you have acted differently? What would have influenced your decision?

Pop Quiz!

1. How did the Indian Partition influence the state of the country?
2. When did the Indian Constitution come into being?
3. How is the Indian political system organized?
4. How do you convey India's role in the world?

Chapter 6 - Indian Culture and Religion

India has a rich heritage and culture. One of its primary characteristics is *unity,* in the sense that people from different races, religions, speaking various languages and adepts of distinct faiths have recognized the importance of spiritual and ethical values.

Generally speaking, Indian people are tolerant, peace-loving and devoted to God. One of the fundamental guiding principles is *Dharma,* which teaches that everyone, irrespective of social status and gender is bound to it.

Additionally, the ethical values of the Indians are illustrated in the Indian Constitution, which is based on secularism. It esteems all religions and faiths, and it doesn't favor any religious belief over another one. It doesn't reckon any distinctions based on race, religion, caste or sex since spiritual beings are made equal.

The Indian civilization has developed based on moral and religious values. This is where its strength and unity is derived from. The Indian ethical systems and philosophy have been strongly influenced by religion.

The Hindu Perception on Life

We couldn't talk about the Hindu culture as being something unchanging, fixed or static. On the opposite, it is continually changing and evolving, adapting itself to the conditions, responding to fresh challenges and assimilating ideas. That is reflected in the existence of various religious reforms during the centuries, which played a major role in the development of the Indian society.

Another crucial element is that the Hindu culture is tolerant when it comes to doctrinal differences, and it approaches subjects such as truth and knowledge from a liberal angle.

Furthermore, the Hindu culture is quintessentially ethical and spiritual. The man is a spiritual being, and he has an innate awareness of spiritual nature regarding the universe. A man's soul, consciousness, and mind constitute essential elements. By embracing discipline and knowledge, the man can aim at controlling his desires, in this way subordinating them.

The Hindu culture highlights the utmost significance of implementing physical, moral, spiritual and mental discipline practices. These are crucial as they help him to comprehend the nature of God and the universe. These cannot be apprehended through a rational process, but through meditation, intuition and contemplation.

Moreover, acquiring wealth or addressing the needs of the senses aren't conveyed as fundamental aims in life. On the contrary, the most important goals are spiritual freedom and righteousness. Still, this doesn't mean that it condemns attaining wealth, as long as these don't degenerate in sensuality, greed and lack of self-control.

Hinduism promotes organizing social life in four different castes. In essence, the caste system depends on an individual's temperament, his vocation, and personal traits. Everyone must take on the responsibilities of his office and unselfishly perform them, waiting for God's reward according to his actions. A man's duties depend on the period of his life, and this information is included in the sacred commentaries and books.

On that note, first of all, a man should develop his mental, physical and spiritual discipline and strength. Secondly, he should take on the responsibility of a householder, wishing to sustain other people, being encouraged by an innate sense of duty. Thirdly, one should take on the journey of self-renunciation, contemplation, and meditation. And lastly, he must humanity with the benefits of having accomplished spiritual and intellectual maturity.

The key to the Hindu culture's imperishability and longevity is determined by its tolerance, intellectual humility, and thorough understanding of the nature of man. It highlights that a human being has a spiritual soul.

This perception on life prevails until today, influencing the lives of millions of people. The Hindu culture has survived the centuries, and it remains dynamic and influential.

As we already pointed, India is the land of diversity, Hinduism being among the oldest religions that took birth in the region. Jainism, Buddhism, Sikhism, Islam, and Christianity are other widespread beliefs on Indian Territory.

The Influence of Islam on the Indian Culture

Islam has contributed significantly to the Indian culture. As we have seen in the first chapters, the Muslims have invaded India gradually, in this way implementing a range of their religious beliefs and customs. Islam's faith in monotheism and equality of all men significantly influenced the Hindu way of thinking. The majority of the Muslim population living in India is indigenous, and their culture and society were influenced by the Hindus as well.

In other words, Islam contributed to Hinduism by simplifying its elaborate rituals and placing the focus on the importance of equality between men. During the time of Akbar – The Great Mughal, Muslims, and Hindus used to take part in their religious and social festivals. This indicates how these two religions have enriched one another.

The Impact of the British Rule on the Indian Culture

The British aimed at changing the Indian society from the inside out, alienating the Indian individual from its national identity. Imminently, many Indians were drawn to the new culture, which promoted a new religion as well – Christianity. Thus, many Indians were converted to Christianity.

The Core of Indian Culture

The Vedic lifestyle represents the heart and soul of the Indian culture. As long as this spiritual perception of life prevails, India will not only survive but will flourish. Sometimes, traditions could appear distorted, especially after a given timeframe, due to deviations and incursions. Nevertheless, as long as the emphasis is directed on the soul, this culture will keep on living, readapting itself depending on the individual needs of the people.

Buddhism in Indian Culture

Siddhartha Gautama, the founder of Buddhism, was born approximately around 563 BCE. His family was wealthy. Nevertheless, he didn't enjoy living a life of privilege, rejecting it. Instead, he preferred adopting a lifestyle of *asceticism* – namely severe self-discipline. After spending 49 consecutive days meditating, he became the Buddha, or *the Enlightened one*. He publicly affirmed that in 528 BCE. Consequently, a group of disciples followed him, who eventually became Buddhist monks. They traveled all around northern India in order to spread these teachings.

Buddhism features a pregnant individualistic element, indicating that each person is responsible for his/her own happiness. The Buddhist way of life presented four noble truths. Life has suffering, the root of suffering is desire, putting an end to desire or controlling it equals ending suffering. Hence, in order to accomplish these goals, one has to follow the Noble Eightfold Path: embracing the right belief, speech, resolve, conduct, and mindfulness. So, following these practices could aid one to be freed from samsara – the cycle of suffering and rebirth.

Apart from that, Buddhism disregarded the caste system. As a result, it was much more appealing to the lower castes. Buddhism indicated that each has the possibility of accomplishing enlightenment in his/her life. Apart from that, according to Buddhism, the one's place in society wasn't a punishment for actions committed in the past.

Furthermore, women were enabled to get more involved, as well, since they could become Buddhist monks if they wished. In other words, this religion gave them the opportunity of escaping their typical sphere of occupation.

It goes without saying that following the eightfold path wasn't an effortless task. As a result, Buddhism wasn't quite popular with merchants or servants who didn't have the time and energy to attain those goals. As a result, Buddhist leaders established a new form of Buddhism, known as *Mahayana Buddhism,* which allowed people to accomplish enlightenment by performing acts of devotion or simply doing their jobs respectfully. Consequently, this made Buddhism more accessible.

At the end of his long life, the Buddha outlined the seven principles by which a society could flourish. Some of them are maintaining and respecting the existing festivals, rituals, and pilgrimages, and honoring holy men. The festivals he referred to were primary Vedic. Calling Buddha a revolutionary could be an exaggeration, both in social and religious matters. He wasn't a rebel. On the opposite, he wanted the existing customs of Hinduism to continue.

Buddhist buildings in India featured the designs of the Vedic habitat. Also, Buddhist temple conventions still followed a well-established Hindu pattern. As for the Buddhist mantras, they were similar to the typical Vedic mantras.

That being said, it could be argued that Buddhism still preserved Hinduism, at its core.

However, due to the Islamic invasion, the spread of Buddhism was almost stopped. The expansion of Buddhism depended almost exclusively on the Buddhist monks, who used to study at the Indian universities from that time. With the coming of the Muslim, most universities were destroyed and many Buddhist monks were killed. As for their libraries, they were burnt as well. On that note, the only places in which Buddhism survived were the ones in which the Islamic invaders didn't venture, such as the North East, the Himalayan region of Leh, Tibet, Ladakh, and so on.

Distinct from Hinduism, Buddhism was mainly concentrated in Buddhist institutions. As for Hinduism, it was spread among the people in both villages and towns. What is more, the Buddhist ideal was a high purpose, which made it difficult to achieve. In that sense, it could be argued that Buddhism was elitist in both practice and philosophy; this prevented it from being widely accessible to the average man.

Jainism

Jainism is another ancient religion that originates from India, similar to Hinduism and Buddhism. Even though it has some things in common with both Hinduism and Buddhism, Jainism is distinct in the sense that it emphasizes asceticism and complete non-violence.

This form of religion took birth in the 6th century BCE, at the same time when Buddhism was developing. That was a time of religious renewal, when several groups and individuals started to condemn the hierarchical organization and formalized rituals associated with traditional Hinduism, looking for something new and more rewarding, which didn't discriminate as much.

Nevertheless, it is worth noting that, similar to Buddhism, Jainism also has its roots in Hinduism, although there are numerous differences between them, as well. The core of the

Jain belief is the spiritual and material realm. It is believed that these realities are both eternal and that human beings can engage in both, and their acts and decisions have consequences.

In Jainism, the soul is eternal, and it has never ending knowledge and power. Still, they believe that it is not created. On the opposite, it has the inherited potential of the divinity, being omniscient, omnipotent and free. Notwithstanding, it is not the equivalent of a god.

In Indian philosophy, karma is conveyed as being the natural moral law imposed by the universe in which both bad and good actions and decisions have corresponding consequences. That would explain why some people are rich; others are poor, others are lucky, pretty, skilled, talented, and so on. Karma is also believed to be one of the preliminary factors that influence the form one takes when he/she is born. *Good karma* would equal high spiritual state, great physical state; on the opposite side, *bad karma* would result in negative spiritual and physical state.

Varying by one's spirituality level and karma, death could mean being reborn and taking another physical appearance on Earth, joining other free souls in heaven or suffering punishment in one of the eight hells. Distinct from the hell imagery that is typical of most religions, the eight hells presented in Jainism become progressively colder. Additionally, suffering isn't eternal. Once the soul is punished for its actions, it will be reborn in another form.

Misconceptions

1. The Vedas Worship Many Gods and Goddesses

Another common misconception is that Hinduism is a polytheistic religion that worships numerous gods. Nevertheless, the Vedas concentrate on worshipping the one and only Paramatma, who is omnipotent and omnipresent.

Thereupon, the human mind is limited and cannot grasp its attributes and qualities.

That being said, the Vedas encompass prayers to the one and only Paramatma, concentrating on distinct attributes and adjectives.

Apart from that, another source of confusion is assuming that Paramatma is synonymous with Devata. Devata refers to someone or something that illuminates, enlightens, or gives something valuable. That's why, in various circumstances, Paramatma could also be perceived as Devata.

But this applies to other inanimate objects that meet the requirements of Devata. On that note, Devatas do deserve to be respected since they provide us with a wide range of selfless benefits. Notwithstanding, that doesn't make Devatas the goal of our worship, which makes the distinction between them and Paramatma.

Moreover, distinct Hindu practices allow different representations of God. But each of these representations (Deva) is merely a depiction of God. That's because the Hindus reckon that one supreme God cannot be truly comprehended by the human mind. Hence, early representations such as Vishnu, Shiva, and others have a symbolic meaning, representing a far-reaching God.

That being said, the Hindus convey God from a complex perspective. They also acknowledge that each person can understand it differently. Still, all these representations revolve around a supreme God.

2. Yoga Is an Exercising System

Yoga was created in order to offer both physical and mental nourishment. Yoga is an ancient tradition, which has been preserved by hermits and scientists. It was renowned for its therapeutic qualities, as it was widely utilized by hermits, who used to roam from place to place, meditating. Although it's true that yoga promotes physical exercise, its primary goal is in fact to accomplish self-discipline.

The term yoga comes from the Sanskrit word "yok Tra", which means a yoke.

Approximately 2,100 years ago, the foundations of yoga were first set. People believed that the human body encompassed channels known as Nadi and centers named Chakra. In the event in which those are blocked, the energy inside the body is trapped, and cannot be released. The release of energy facilitates the body to accomplish many powers that are typically beyond its capability.

In ancient times, teaching yoga was a fundamental segment of the traditional form of education.

The significance and meaning of yoga was lost in translation. The information that reached our ears is mostly a Western interpretation of yoga, which doesn't grasp its full connotation. That being said, yoga is renowned as one of the six schools of Hinduism.

Concurrently, it adheres to the *Advaita* tradition. That refers to the belief in one consciousness, one truth, and everything the deity stands for. Apart from the seeming duality of life, this remains 100 percent true. Hence, the primary purpose of yoga is to still and calm your mind so that you can become fully aware of this truth, and live your life accordingly.

The classical system of yoga, known as Raja Yoga, acknowledges eight distinct limbs. One of these is *asana,* also referred to the physical practice of postures. So, what is the primary purpose of the postures? That is to create and to keep the body healthy, so that it could follow the other limbs, including meditation.

That's because meditation is among the most important tools

that enable one to accomplish the awareness of truth.

3. Hinduism Is Just a Religion

Hinduism is renowned as one of the world's oldest religions, having approximately one billion followers. Thus, Hinduism is the third largest religion in the world. Notwithstanding, this is so much more than a religion, as most people perceive it.

The foundation of Hinduism is lost in time, being argued by specialists. The earliest form of Hindu scripture, namely the Rig Veda, is assumed to have been composed before 6,500 BC. What is more, the word Hinduism cannot be found in their scriptures. This name was given by the Persians, who used to occupy the area between the rivers Hindu and Sindh.

That being said, Hinduism represents much more than a form of religion. It is a way of living. In essence, it is a conglomeration of distinct philosophical, religious and cultural beliefs, ideas and traditions that have evolved in time.

Apart from that, a common misconception regarding Hinduism is that adepts worship cows. This assumption is vastly determined by the way in which Hindus convey and treat this animal. They reckon that the cow gives more than it takes, being, in fact, a symbol of other animals, as well. Essentially, the cow stands for the sustenance of life. It takes water, grass, and gray, and, in exchange, it provides us with milk, cheese, yogurt, cream, fertilizer for the fields. That's why it *gives more than it takes*.

Furthermore, cows are respected due to their gentle nature. From an outsider's perspective, it may appear as if the Hindus venerate the cow, but in fact, they just honor and respect all animals.

Fun Facts!
- Hinduism is known as *Sanatana Dharma,* whose significance is eternal dharma, or eternal truth.
- Hindus believe in reincarnation. They acknowledge that the soul is immortal and it can take numerous forms until it accomplishes ultimate enlightenment.
- The Vedas were preserved for approximately 5,000 years without utilizing the print. That was achieved by memorization.

If It Were Your Choice
As we did in the previous chapters, I provoke you to put yourself in the shoes of Siddhartha Gautama, the founder of Buddhism. Would you have continued living a life of privilege or you would have challenged your thinking in order to accomplish something greater? Why? Consider the social context, as well.

Pop quiz!
1. What is the connection between the Indian culture and secularism?
2. What are some of the main principles of the Hindu way of living?
3. What are other prevalent religions on the Indian Territory?
4. In what way did Islam impact Hinduism and why?
5. Why did Buddhism attract the lower castes?

Chapter 7 - Delhi + Things to See in India

Visiting India is definitely a unique experience. It is a vibrant, colorful country of unimaginable contrasts where you'll see the traditional and the modern meet and blend unexpectedly. Its rich heritage is mirrored in the diversity it offers. During the centuries, several cultures have left their mark on the Indian culture – this is visible today.

Delhi

Delhi is a testament to India's uniqueness in diversity. Here, time travel is an attainable purpose. Your time machine is the metro, which can take you from Old Delhi, where time appears to have stayed still, to New Delhi, where you'll find grand parliament buildings dating from the colonial era.

Delhi is a vibrating metropolis whose population is bigger than Australia's. It is one of the main cities in India whose historical roots have remained intact in spite of becoming a commercial metropolis.

The Red Fort represents an emblematic icon of India, receiving this name due to its impressive sandstone walls that used to encircle the Mughal Empire. The building was first constructed in 1648, being a fortified palace, serving as the capital of the empire. This is a majestic building due to the exquisite architectural details and historical importance.

The Qutub Minar is another notable attraction based in India. It is acknowledged as the second tallest minaret in the country. The tower was constructed in order to illustrate victory over Delhi's last Hindu empire. On the setting, you'll also find the first Islamic mosque in India, and a few gardens and ruins surrounding it. The bazaars of old Delhi, together with the mouthwatering foods are two other reasons why Delhi will offer you a unique traveling experience.

The Taj Mahal, Agra

The Mahal is, without a doubt, one of India's most famous buildings. Apart from that, the symbolic meaning it carries is just as important, being the world's most renowned testimony to the importance and power of love. It was built for Mumtaz Mahal, the beloved wife of Emperor Shah Jahan – after her death.

The building incorporates stunning elements of Islamic design including minarets, arches, a dome, black calligraphy featuring the entrance to the building. It also has white marble embellished with intricate inlaid floral patterns. Not to mention that it is decorated with precious stones such as diamonds, jades, and other valuable stones.

The Holy City of Varanasi

This city carries major cultural and religious importance for the Hindus, being a significant pilgrimage center. It is often linked to the mighty Ganges River, which represents an important symbol in Hinduism. It dates back to the 8th century, being one of the oldest populated cities in the entire world: it is impressive and breathtaking.

Exploring the old quarter, which is adjacent to the Ganges is a must; there you'll find the majestic Kashi Vishwanath Temple, which was constructed back in 1780. If you want to convey this holy city from a distinct perspective, bathing in the Ganges is an equally unique experience.

The Gateway of India, Mumbai

The Gateway of India overlooks the majestic Arabian Sea, and it is a must see. It was constructed to commemorate the coming of King George the 5th and his wife, Queen Mary in 1911. It is built almost exclusively of concrete and yellow basalt, and the Indo-Saracenic design is, indeed, noteworthy.

Nonetheless, this spot also carries historical importance, since this is the place where the procession of the British soldiers took place in 1948 when India regained its independence.

The Golden City: Jaisalmer

The Golden city of Jaisalmer is a testament of stunning architecture rising from the sand dunes of the Thar Desert. Previously being a strategic outpost, now, the city boasts with beautiful old mansions, grand gateways and the majestic Jaisalmer Fort also referred to as the Golden Fort, which is a structure dating from the 12th century.

Apart from the fine old homes, temples, and unique palaces, the fortress has 99 bastions along the gates, which lead to the primary courtyard where the Maharaja Palace is located. The Palace was built in the early 1500s and was altered for numerous times by successive rulers. As a result, the construction combines a range of fantastic features.

Harmandir Sahib: The Golden Temple in Amritsar

Established in 1577 by Ram Das, this temple is a crucial element in Sikh history and culture. The primary attraction is, of course, the golden temple, also known as Harmandir Sahib. It is considered to be the holiest of India's Sikh shrines, attracting high numbers of Hindus and people of other faiths. The temple represents a terrific blend of Islamic and Hindu styles.

The lower marble section highlights inlaid animal and floral motifs, while the golden dome represents the lotus flower, which is an element symbolizing the purity of the Sikhs. Apart from the terrific architectural design, you're bound to be impressed by the spiritual atmosphere in the temple, effects maximized by the prayers chanted from the holy book of the Sikhs.

Mecca Masjid, Hyderabad

The Mecca Masjid is renowned as one of the oldest and largest mosques based on the Indian Territory, originating from 1614. It is big enough as to accommodate no less than 10,000 worshippers; this beautiful mosque is a feast to the eyes of the beholder.

The impressive complex incorporates the principal gateway, a far-reaching Plaza, a large pond, and a room that keeps the hair of Prophet Mohammed. The inscriptions from the Holy Book featuring some of the arches and doors of the construction are other notable features. The name of the building is inspired by the bricks above the central gate, which had been brought from Mecca.

Pop Quiz!

1. What are some of the main attractions in Delhi?
2. What is the story behind the building of The Taj Mahal?
3. Why should one consider visiting the golden city of Jaisalmer?

Conclusion

India has witnessed a considerable number of military conflicts, from its early beginnings until recently. The coming of Islam in ancient India didn't shatter their culture, which is an early sign of India's approach to tolerance and acceptance. Islam has influenced Hinduism in the way that it made India's religious followers see the faults in their approach, and change what needed to be changed.

The medieval period noted a series of developments in arts, culture, political administration, propelling the country forward. The decline of the Moghul Empire was followed by the British Colonization, which could be conveyed as the English attempt to alienate the locals from their local customs, traditions, and beliefs.

Irrespective of the hardships experienced by the Indians during the colonization period, they never gave up and kept fighting for their independence – a fight that was inspired by great thinkers. Mahatma Gandhi, also known as *the Father of the Nation,* wanted to reunite the country, promoting non-violence and tolerance. After attaining its independence, India kept on fighting to become a self-governed country and rose from the ashes.

India was, and still is, a grand empire, whose smooth voice of an old intelligence teaches us how to live peacefully. Sanskrit could be conveyed as being the mother of Europe's languages, while the Vedas incorporate practical information about medicine, surgery, music and mechanized art.

The Vedas represent India's ancient encyclopedia that covers the most important aspects of life, music, religion, philosophy, cosmology, law, ethics, and science. Schopenhauer himself highlighted that the Vedas is the most elevated and rewarding book in the world.

So, as you can see, India is rich in terms of culture and history:

once you learn about it, you cannot help but be amazed by everything it has to offer.

DEFINITELY THE BEST BOOK CLUB ONLINE...

"If you love books. You will love the Lean Stone Book Club."

*** Exclusive Deals That *Any* Book Fan Would Love! ***

Visit leanstonebookclub.com/join

(AND... IT'S FREE)!

Made in the USA
Middletown, DE
09 February 2018